A Story of Christmas Around the World

THE INTERNATIONAL ELVES

For Zander, Aviana, Cyrus, and Sophia.

I love you dearly and hope you carry the magic with you everyday, not just around Christmas.

Love, Mommy/Khaleh

Paresa Noble

For Ezekiel and Elessia.

Thank you for inspiring me to carry on the Christmas spirit. May you continue to be full of joy and laughter and bring the brightest smiles to everyones faces. I love you both.

Love, Mommy

Selena Mendoza

Every Christmas Eve, Rika and NaiNai were in charge of loading Santa's sleigh with all the gifts for children across the world.

On this particular Christmas Eve, there was a little bit of a hiccup. As Rika loaded up the last gift into Santa's gift bag, she lost her balance.

Plop!

Rika toppled into the back of the sleigh.

NaiNai wanted to help his friend. As he reached down to grab Rika's hand and pull her out, the sleigh jolted forward.

OH NO!

It was time for Santa and his reindeers to start delivering presents.

Rika and NaiNai both peeked over the side of the sleigh to see what happened.

They found themselves flying through the air in Santa's sleigh, with Santa himself leading the way.

"Ahem, Santa Claus?" Rika said in her squeaky voice.

Santa looked back to find Rika and NaiNai sitting bashfully. He let out a warm and familiar laugh.

"Ho, ho, ho – how did you guys get in here?" he asked with a smile on his face.

Rika and NaiNai explained what happened.

"Well, looks like you're going to help me deliver presents! Come join me up front!

Before they knew it, the sleigh zoomed into the Northern Lights.

The next thing they knew, Santa's sleigh was flying low, hovering right above the ocean. The coastline sparkled with lights ahead.

"Australia gets their presents a bit differently than the rest of the world. I like to do it how they do it. Can you hold my hat?" Santa grabbed his surfboard and bag of gifts as he jumped in the water, landing both feet on his surfboard.

He splashed alongside the sleigh as he caught a wave into Sydney's harbor.

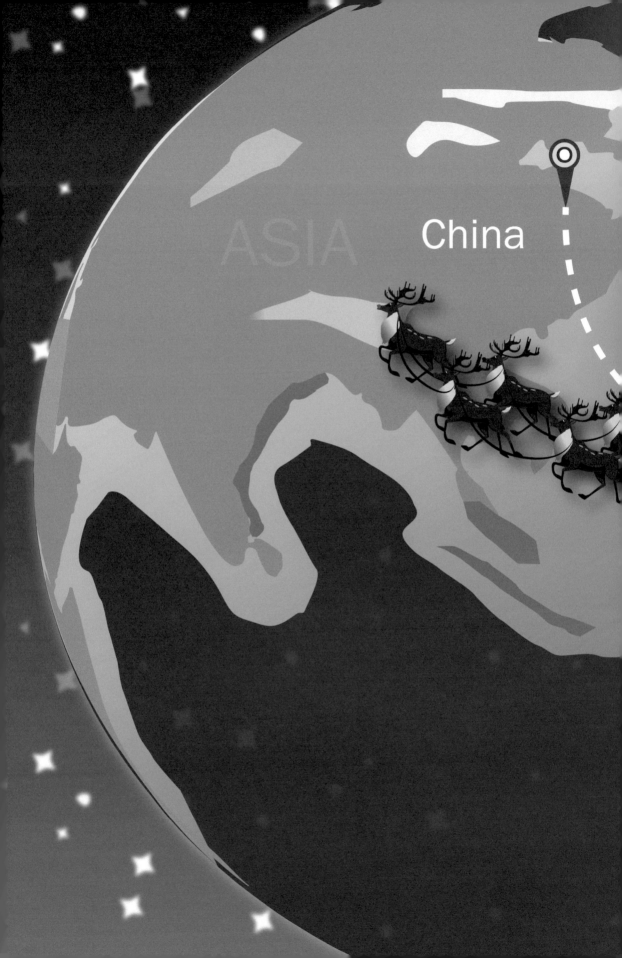

Once they delivered the gifts across Australia, they headed to Asia.

New South Wales

AUSTRALIA

Santa, Rika, and NaiNai visited all around Asia. They went to a city called Shanghai in China and flew from apartment to apartment, from house to house delivering gifts.

In each house Santa went to, he found a beautiful basket of apples. They weren't just any apples – they were peace apples, called Ping Guo in Chinese.

Santa handed a Ping Guo to Rika and NaiNai as they took off from Shanghai.

"Families share and eat these peace apples together on Christmas to bless their family with a safe and peaceful year ahead," he explained. "Next stop, Africa!"

AFRICA

Kenya

Santa's sleigh landed softly in a town called Amani, located in Kenya, Africa. Families were sleeping, resting for a day of celebrations ahead. Outside of each home hung colorful kente cloths that some family members would wear the next day.

Santa smiled as he left gifts for the children under these beautiful cloths.

Once they delivered the gifts across Africa, Santa, Rika, and NaiNai made their way to Europe, visiting houses all along the way.

Santa's sleigh soared through the stars as they visited all of Europe. As they flew over Munich in Germany, Rika and NaiNai were amazed by the beautiful markets lighting up the town below them.

"In Germany, they call me ChristKindl!" Santa said cheerfully as they landed on the roof of the first house.

Santa walked in to find Stollen waiting for him on the table. Stollen is a yummy cake with fruit in it. He took a big bite that put a big smile on his face. "Mmm, that's so delicious!"

After he left the gifts and trinkets under the tree for the kids, Santa bid farewell to the angels and nutcrackers that lined the mantle of the fireplace.

Colorado,
United States of America

North America

Germany

Europe

The sleigh soared over the Atlantic Ocean as Santa, Rika, and NaiNai made their way to North America.

Santa visited all the cities across North America. Rika and NaiNai's favorite place was in Denver, CO. It reminded them of the North Pole because of its tall mountains covered in snow.

Santa went down the chimney into a house with a big beautiful Christmas tree that lit up the dark room, leaving presents for the family to open together on Christmas morning.

Santa found the most delicious cookies on the coffee table, made just for him. He even found some fresh carrots for his reindeer. He took a big bite of the cookie and washed it down with some cold milk before he headed back up the chimney.

Colorado,
United States of America

North America

Santa, Rika, and NaiNai headed south as they made their way to South America.

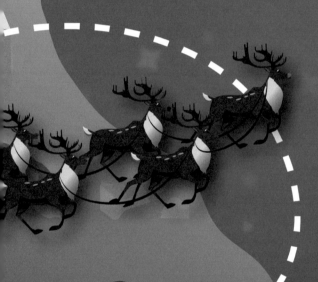

Venezuela

South America

One of the places they visited in South America was Caracas, Venezuela. Rika looked down to see that the streets in the city were blocked off. ◄

"Santa, why are the streets closed?"

"Good question, Rika! In the morning, people in Caracas will wake up, put on their roller skates, and skate through the streets of the city. There are so many people who roller skate at the same time that they close the streets to cars on Christmas morning. That's why they have it blocked off.

Santa, Rika, and NaiNai delivered the final present in South America, and their work was done. All the gifts had been delivered just in time for families to wake up in the morning and enjoy their time together.

It was time for Santa and the elves to fly back to the North Pole.

The next day, families, friends, and loved ones all over the world woke up with joy filling their minds, and love filling their hearts, as they celebrated a Merry Christmas *together.*

Paresa is a loving wife and mama to two adorable kiddos. She works in the world of marketing and writing with her own entrepreneurial flair. At home, it's all about fun family moments, tunes that keep everyone grooving, and delicious food adventures. She's not just running a business; she's living her passions every day, blending work with play, and family with creativity.

Selena combines her graphic design expertise from Northwest Kansas Technical College with her experiences as a loving wife and mother to two sweet little ones. Her passion for reading, nature photography, and family brings life to her illustrations with a unique blend of creativity and warmth, making every design a reflection of her love for storytelling.

Made in the USA
Columbia, SC
16 November 2024

45757632R00027